weekend
millionaires

For Sue ...
Hopefully the next
one won't take me quite
as long!
with loads of love
& thanks for your faith!
support.,
Gareth
Dec '07
x

poetry

gareth jones

tall-lighthouse

for Mum, Dad and Martyn

Acknowledgements:

Thanks to the editors and publishers of the following
publications where some of these poems, or versions
of these poems first appeared: *The Fix, Guardian Unlimited,
New Welsh Review, The New Writer, Reactions 5* and *Seam.*
'Unreel' received third prize in the 2004 Cardiff Academi
International Poetry Competition.

Grateful thanks also go out to Ahren Warner, Camellia
Stafford, James Byrne, Jennifer Copley and Megan Thompson
for invaluable advice on the manuscript; Roddy Lumsden,
for steering a stubborn vessel in the right direction,
Catherine Smith and to Hannah Blake, my biggest fan
and harshest critic.

cover image : mat redvers

cover photo : hannah blake

tall-lighthouse pilot publication - new poetry
from young poets - series edited by Roddy Lumsden
and supported by Arts Council England

ISBN 978-1-904551-35-5
tall-lighthouse
www.tall-lighthouse.co.uk

contents

*... when a man in a forest thinks he is going
in a straight line, in reality he is going
in a circle... I did my best to go in a circle,
hoping in that way to go in a straight line.*

Samuel Beckett, Molloy

Unreel

Strung along the street one morning
       like low-level bunting; a mystery

to passing dogs who nose along it:
       a length of cassette tape looped and wound

across a maze of roads to the park –
       a contour, an isobar, brought to life –

straight for a huddle of trees where it rides
       wire-taut around the branches:

something unwelcome, something wrong –
       a crime-scene cordon in a country field,

a deep, dark string of gut gone dry;
       it rasps like an army of plastic bags

but cannot disclose the secrets it holds:
       the dead notes of a discarded LP

or a long-gone listened-to radio programme,
       a declaration of love, a confession,

someone's last words, the half-deranged sermon
       that could have saved us all, or simply

the pure grey noise of tape-head static –
       the silence of something about to be said

A-Z

'A man who, beyond the age of 26, finds himself on a bus can count himself as a failure.' attr. Margaret Thatcher

I claim it as my morning prize:
top deck, pavement side, the last-but-one seat,
barricading my space with rucksack and jacket
as the schoolkids jostle their way up the stairs:
the keen ones choosing the front and the view,
the cooler ones herding towards the back row.

What's next is all mapped out for them
beyond the tags on the seat-backs and cushions,
the initials scratched on the windows with coins,
the way they will lose their desire to be *seen*,
resting their heads, instead, on the glass
at an earlier, darker, hour than this,

adding to the smears on the panes
where nameless scalps have left their mark -
the grime and grease of honest work -
losing themselves in tabloids or daydreams,
while buses follow familiar patterns
and the city around them shifts and fattens.

The Other Side

A litany of names not even whispered
in the darkest corners of the village playground:
those daughters and sons whose eyes were too wide,
who laughed or waved their hands, and strode
the banks between the surf and quicksand,
who talked of a place the other side.

This is all I know for certain:
there are women here who spend their days
staring from their hearths towards the net curtains
as if expecting a familiar face;
and men who wander the length of the sea wall,
their faces lined by drink and the spray,
who sleep badly with the wind at the door,
who will not and cannot say why.

Breakage

She compared it to the wine glass you broke
        at Easter last year:
how you plucked it up from the draining board
        and the precious bulb
shattered in your hand, ribboning your palm;
        how she can't forget
the way you stood there silenced, as the blood
        trickled down your arm.

She knew full well it was the same glass she
        had caught with the pan
just minutes before – expecting a crack
        that never sounded –
and held the small wonder up to the light,
        amazed at its strength;
how it seemed to come from nowhere,
        like sickness, or love.

Turning Point

A pigeon-face peers out from a hole
in the brickwork over a gable-end window.
A sudden cold descends, waves of static
make aerials, power lines chirrup and click.

Like dangling mittens, two trainers sway
on a telegraph wire. And *now* comes the rain
at the place where, displaced by buses and cars,
the tarmac laps at the pavement's shore.

The hard edge of the storm meets the middle
of the carriageway. Overnight, a puddle
in the turning point will broil thickly with fish;
morels and ceps will grace the woodchip
of the central reservation; wild rocket
will pepper the green of the roundabout.

Fit

In the same way
the key we had cut from a cut key
sometimes rolls in the lock,

and no pair of earphones
quite sits in my earlobes,
or the way the clock

you hung in the kitchen
the night we moved in
has never looked right,

and no suit
I've bought
seems to make me look smart,

what would be the sense
in fooling ourselves,
when we are only

as made for each other
as two winsome lovers
in a twelfth century

village, its boundary wall
the edge of the known world;
when harmony is simply

a state of waiting
for one of the dueting
musicians to stray?

There would be no passion
without frustration,
no taming without the wild.

So give me the struggle,
the heat and the trouble.
Give us a wayward child.

Home

Each evening we go back to it,
   like the rut of a worn-out argument:

the double helix of dirty dishes;
   the clot of smalls in the washing machine;

mirrors that lay bare our laughter lines,
   though the joke is long forgotten;

cupboards and drawers, their paraphernalia
   evidence of our years:

a mug-ringed photo of a Shropshire village;
   ticket stubs, petty foreign change;

nursery paintings by nephews and nieces;
   the clothes and toys we never needed;

a creased and yellowed note that says:
   I love you so much. Please stay.

Here

Morning arrives with unwilling acceptance,
the sky the colour of an artist's brushwater.

In the field by the river, two burnt-out cars
shed flakes of ash into the breeze.

An angler's hook snags suddenly tight;
his line protests against the weight.

Not far from here, a mobile phone
trills into an empty room.

Elsewhere, beneath a man's easy manner,
the hard facts are being ring-fenced.

The Gloom

It rubbed off on the Friday collections:
red bills, rent cheques and re-directed
circulars; wedding invitations
and RSVPs; competition entries;
begging letters; job applications...

Mailbags collapsed like cooling towers
in the backs of knackered hi-top vans,
trains that grumbled through the hours
towards dawn, beyond the city postcodes,
through darkened, sleeping country towns.

As workers on shifts slunk wordlessly home,
early risers slipped back to bed,
joggers postponed their morning runs,
and parents ignored, as best they could,
their teething babies' sullen grizzling.

Families turned away from each other,
not even able to face themselves:
breakfasts, if eaten, were silent affairs.
Cats and dogs sought out their baskets.
Cows went unmilked, milk undelivered.

By lunchtime, it had reached the sea:
funfairs looked no fun at all;
piers were peered at from grimy cafés
by doleful couples playing with snacks,
nursing flat pints or mugs of thin tea.

Daytrippers felt suddenly homesick;
weekend millionaires were spent.
Waves lapped greyly over the sandbanks;
a milky sun half-tried a smile,
was nowhere near enough, and sank.

To the Rose-ringed Parakeet

The acid green of a Post-it Note,
lemon 'n' lime, a child's crayoned grass,

the neon shock of your tree-clipping squadrons
shakes carnival into a beige afternoon;

your *unoiled-wheel-on-a-wheelbarrow* screech has
me running to the window.

Escapee from a cagebird dealer,
quarantine holding at Heathrow airport,

or Shepperton Studios movie set,
passing migrant that decided to linger:

whatever the truth of what brought you here
from the verdant foothills of the Himalayas,

may you colour these drab city skies forever
with your raucous squawk and emerald shimmer.

The Streaker

How he jerks the crowd awake,
cracking his joke at the sunless day
with the pasty, cellulit-moon of his arse,
fat cock knocking against his legs
in an almost perfect figure-of-eight,
unkempt hair unleashed to the breeze.

So graceful in his gracelessness,
face aglow, he absorbs the applause
and laughter, arms aloft to our cheers –
this butt-naked clown, reclaiming the buff
of bedroom and shower for the public domain,
for all of us choked in our man-made fibres.

He jinks and steps with a scrum-half's toes,
leaves a steward face-down in his wake
and, with a final, triumphant cartwheel,
he escapes into the crowd, a hero.
Though almost as one, we pull our coats
upwards, tight around our throats.

Farm

Last night you came to me in a dream,

and so I followed the fishless brook

through the wood – where bluebells no longer

grow, but year-round death caps prosper –

along the edge of the blight-ruined field

towards the silent, fire-scorched yard –

where we slaughtered the last of the calves,

the night he swore he was out of our lives –

to the gaping mouth of the barn, and the loop

of rope slung over the beam.

Teacher

Even now it takes so little:
the faintest whiff of bleach on the stairwell,
a hacking cough a floor or two up.
You know the day is a bad one when you
well up at the sight of his dictionary.

And so the red-haired waitress at the diner
sees something in your face that worries her
and busies herself scrubbing the table-tops.
Steering her way around your booth,
she doesn't look up when you leave.

You drift from there to the edge of town,
to the slum blocks, the burnt-out garbage-cans,
where no one knows who he was or cares,
but an old woman offers you a cigarette,
as though she knows something of your burden,

the shadow stretching ahead of you.
'All those long afternoons in the classroom,'
he said that day, 'Was *this* all they were for?'
Some evenings you listen to kids in the street
and tell yourself you're not waiting for him.

The Ex

is an unsurpable god:
a figure you cannot scorn or murder,
or betray with your embrace.

is a stubborn phantom,
a shadow skirting your peripheral vision,
lording familiar paths of carpet.

is bedded-in among
her possessions, the everyday et cetera,
subtle as the scar on a Siamese twin.

is the thief who frittered
the years she could not imagine you:
a life she would not have had you part of.

is the one she thinks back to,
in the syrup dark, the face she paints,
the flesh she sculpts on to yours.

will succeed in the end,
leering by the bed, those tense, cold nights
you cannot reach her, sneering at your rows,

knowing well how all this leads
to that last, dull click of the front door,
and you becoming him.

There

So out of place at this time of morning,
last night's blue chiffon welling around her,
she gifts a few seconds of glamour to anglers
arranging their rigs by the river.

As she hurries by the derelict glassworks
that hasn't a window left in place,
she thinks of the boy at the club last night,
who had *his* smell, *his* troubled face,
and grips the three small coins in her fist.
Today she may need to be brave.

When she reaches the main road, even the sight
of the monkey puzzle tree cannot lift her.
She prises open the phone box. From memory
she starts to dial the number.

The Ajar

Seconds after the buzzer's rasp
your boyish face slots into the ajar,
smileless behind the latch. The sound
of unlocking, then you usher me past
the dark red stain on the threadbare carpet,
the black smudge on the skirting board.

I linger on the roll of your arse,
the V of your back, the swish of your hair,
your fingers gripping the plastic doorknob,
as you guide me through with a glance:
straight to my belt, undoing my trousers,
holding my gaze as you slip off your top.

Already I'm wishing that this was over
and we were clothed, as if we'd just met,
as though nothing much has even happened,
but for the hard facts of crumpled covers,
the room's unmistakable *eau de toilette*,
the lover's notes in my outstretched hand.

The Spare Key

The flat is a state. You open the windows
and begin by collecting his clothes.
Cramming a load in the washer-drier,
you dump the rest in a laundry sack.
Leaving bowls and plates in the sink to soak,
you take on the lounge, black bin bags in hand.
In go the ashtrays, the tikka masala
still sitting in its tray, a stray scrap of naan,
the shredded remains of a chocolate wrapper,
a *very* dead plant, an array of drinks cans,
two *Sunday Sports* (you leave an *Observer*),
the magazine stash beneath the settee.

Sluicing the toilet and shining the taps,
you scrub down the tiles and gather up
the empty bottles of shampoo and shower-gel,
changing his toothbrush, his plastic razor.
You locate the nugget in foil, the *Rizlas*,
re-unite tapes and CDs with cases,
slip paperbacks into gaps on the bookshelf,
sift junk from bank and credit card statements
and introduce carpet to vacuum cleaner.
The kitchen mopped, you examine the contents
of the fridge: a cling-filmed lump of cheddar,
three bottles of *Beck's*, a blueberry muffin.

You drop fresh vegetables into the crisper,
a carton of apple juice into the door.
Wiping the plates and letting them drain,
you leave a mug and bowl to one side –
the breakfast things he'd have left behind.
Knocking back one of the beers, then two,
you sit on the lino, as it starts to sink in,
no longer sure this was the right thing to do,
though his mother is just a day away
and, granted, it's far too late to stop now.
By lunchtime tomorrow the bins will be empty
and she will have had the son she wanted.

Duvet Day

A full moon gracing the afternoon;
two swifts sweeping the sky alone.

The cast-off heap of yesterday's clothes;
the patient alarm awaiting its hour.

The ripple of light that spills through the curtains;
the air misted gold with the dust of two fools.